Drug Culture

ANDREA CLAIRE HARTE SMITH

W
FRANKLIN WATTS
LONDON•SYDNEY

First published in 2003 by Franklin Watts
96 Leonard Street, London EC2A 4XD

Franklin Watts Australia
45-51 Huntley Street
Alexandria, NSW 2015

Copyright © Franklin Watts 2003
Series editor: Rachel Cooke
Series design: White Design
Picture research: Diana Morris

A CIP catalogue record for this book is available from the British Library.

ISBN: 0 7496 4881 3

Printed in Belgium

Acknowledgements:
Bojan Bacelj/Still Pictures: 12c; Philip Bayle/Still Pictures: 21;
David Bebber/Rex Features: 22b; Cesare Bonazza/Rex Features: 19b;
Paul Brown/Rex Features: 20; Nigel Dickinson/Still Pictures: 4, 8b;
Steve Eason/Photofusion: front cover, 17, 26; Colin Edwards/Photofusion: 6 (posed by model);
Michael Freeman/Corbis: 15t; Ron Giling/Still Pictures: 13t; Peter Granser/Still Pictures: 28;
David Hoffman/Still Pictures: 16b; Jeremy Horner/Corbis: 18;
Michael Jenner/Robert Harding PL: 12bl; Andrew Laenen/Rex Features: 11;
Jim McDonald/Corbis: 25; Tristan O'Neill/PYMCA: 24b;
Warren Powell/Photofusion: 5; Thomas Raupach/Still Pictures: 16t;
Rex Features: 9, 19t, 22t, 29; Harmut Schwarzbach/Still Pictures: 8t;
Ian Simpson/Photofusion: 7; Sipa Press/Rex Features: 14, 15b, 23, 24t, 27t;
Alex Smalles/Photofusion: 27b; Camilla Wallberg/Still Pictures: 10.

Whilst every attempt has been made to clear copyright should there be any inadvertent
omission please apply in the first instance to the publisher regarding rectification.

CONTENTS

DRUG CULTURE

THIRTY YEARS AGO, *pupils used to sneak behind bike sheds to have a cigarette. Now some pupils are sneaking off to smoke cannabis instead – and they are trying other drugs too. For many it seems illegal drugs have entered our everyday culture.*

All-night dances – raves – have been criticised for promoting a drug culture because many party-goers take ecstasy.

LEGAL OR ILLEGAL

Two drugs – alcohol and tobacco – have been an accepted part of Western culture for a long time and, just like heroin, they are addictive and life-threatening. The difference is that tobacco and alcohol are legal in Western countries. So why do people risk getting in trouble with the police, as well as their health and even their lives, by taking illegal drugs?

IT FEELS GOOD

Perhaps the best way to understand why people take drugs is to hear some of the positive experiences people have had as a result. Writer Matthew Collin wrote after taking ecstasy with his friend for the first time: "I understood his faults, his hopes, his dreams, his pain and joy, what he had been through ... and I knew that he felt the same." This is similar to the feeling '60s writer Allen Ginsberg had when he first took magic mushrooms: "We're going to teach people to stop hating... Start a peace and love movement."

A NEW PERSPECTIVE

People see the world differently when they take drugs. Drugs can make life seem funnier, more exciting. Drugs can make people lose their shyness or forget their sadness. Michelle Pickthall, a teenage addict, said heroin made her feel: "Warm, relaxed, snuggled up in a hundred comfort blankets. It made me forget everything, made everything go away." But this is only half of the story – the up-side. The down-side is the reason why drugs and drug-use is one of the biggest issues facing both governments and individuals in our world today.

⬇ *Would you be surprised if today's bored teenagers smoked cannabis?*

GET THE FACTS STRAIGHT

- 13% of Australians aged over 14 had used cannabis in the past year (2001 survey), down 7% on 1998.
- Almost 19% of US 18- to 25-year-olds used drugs in 2001, an increase of 3% from the previous year. The number of people who had tried ecstasy for the first time tripled between 1998 and 2000.
- In New Zealand, use of several drugs including marijuana (cannabis leaves), cocaine and heroin stayed level from 1998-2001, but use of ecstasy, amphetamine, methamphetamine and ketamine increased.
- In 1999, cannabis was tried by 26% of 15- to 16-year-olds in Denmark, 24% in the United Kingdom (UK), 23% in Ireland and 7% in Portugal.
- Amphetamines, ecstasy and cocaine have been tried by about 1 to 6% of young adults in the European Union (EU). The UK figures are higher: amphetamine 16% and ecstasy 8%.
- There is a difference between experimenting and regular use: 20% of 15- to 64-year-olds in the EU have tried illegal drugs, but as few as 4% have used them in the past month.

THE DOWN-SIDE

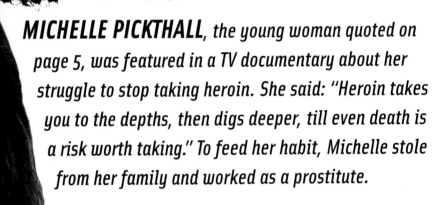

MICHELLE PICKTHALL, *the young woman quoted on page 5, was featured in a TV documentary about her struggle to stop taking heroin. She said: "Heroin takes you to the depths, then digs deeper, till even death is a risk worth taking." To feed her habit, Michelle stole from her family and worked as a prostitute.*

ADDICTED

This is because drugs like heroin can cause a physical addiction so that you feel very ill if you stop taking them. Users can also become reliant on them emotionally, finding it hard to cope without them when things go wrong. "Even when you've been off [heroin] for years, it's still nestling there in your emotional vocabulary, just waiting for you to slip up, anticipating your next relationship breakdown or bereavement," writes author Irvine Welsh, who used to take heroin.

DESPERATION

These effects make addicts so desperate that, like Michelle, they turn to crime – about a third of all theft and burglary in the UK is thought to be drug-related. The drug takes first place in addicts' lives. They will share needles (used to inject heroin) with people and so risk catching serious diseases like HIV, which causes AIDS and hepatitis B and C. They suffer from general ill-health and have more accidents as a result of their drug use.

Drug addicts' lives become a desperate struggle to ensure that they get their next fix.

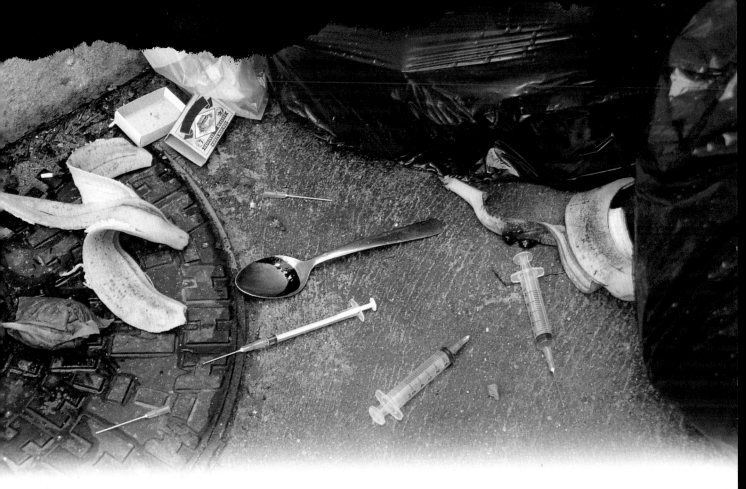

A SAFER OPTION?

People who use ecstasy regularly see it as a safer, non-addictive option, but it may cause brain damage in the long-term, and a single overdose can be fatal. US teenager Danielle Heird died after taking two ecstasy tablets. Cannabis, the most common illegal drug, harms the lungs in the same way as tobacco and can cause feelings of panic. Heavy users can come to rely on it and, according to some sources, face withdrawal symptoms when they stop.

EVERYONE PAYS

These problems are faced by the individual drug user, but there are wider consequences. Governments struggle to find effective, voter-friendly policies to tackle drugs, while its tax payers foot the bill for policing them and the health care needed as a result of drug use. People living in areas where drug misuse is heavy may also live in fear of drug-related crime and worry about their safety and that of their family.

⬆ *Needles discarded by drug addicts are a health risk, particularly to children who might try to play with them.*

WHAT DO YOU THINK?

Many people are worried about the extent that school pupils come into contact with drugs.

- Are people right to be concerned? What do you think about the use of illegal drugs?
- Have you ever been offered drugs?
- Would you tell a parent or teacher if you had used drugs?
- What sort of problems do you think your school or other schools face as a result of drug use?

DRUGS ARE USED in medicines to treat illness, but the word is also applied to chemicals people take to change their mood, give them energy, or make them better at sports. Drugs are anything from a cup of coffee to crack-cocaine.

A street child in Honduras sniffs glue, a depressant.

TOLERANCE LEVELS

If a drug is taken regularly, the body gets used to it and more of the drug has to be taken to get the same effect. A normal dose of heroin or morphine for a long-term addict may be enough to kill a first-time user. An alcoholic may be able to drink a whole bottle of spirits - enough to make most drinkers very sick. Drugs can be natural, such as cannabis and magic mushrooms, or made in a laboratory or factory, for example, ecstasy and alcohol.

THE EFFECTS

There are broadly four categories of effect that people get from illegal drug use.

Depressants dull pain. They relax people and make them feel sleepy. But the body can slow down to such an extent that breathing stops.

Stimulants make users full of energy, chatty and happy. They can increase the heart rate and blood pressure, sometimes to dangerous levels.

Hallucinogens change the way that things look and sound, but this can be in an exciting or a frightening way, depending on who is taking the drug and their state of mind. It can be like living out a nightmare or a fantastic dream.

ENHANCING PERFORMANCE

The fourth category contains the drugs mainly used in sport. These drugs can be used illicitly to increase muscle size in body-building, and to develop strength and speed in sports generally. Sportspeople who have been taking a banned substance sometimes use other drugs, diuretics, to flush the banned drugs out of their system before they are tested by their sport's governing body.

← *A handful of laboratory-made "designer" drugs.*

↓ *A man smokes crack-cocaine, a powerful stimulant.*

COMMON KILLERS

THE WORDS "DRUG USER" *conjure up the picture of a pale, dark-eyed youth, injecting heroin in a grimy bedsit, but drug users are mostly found in pubs, with a glass in one hand and a cigarette in the other.*

SMOKERS COUGH

Tobacco and alcohol have a far bigger impact on health and lifespan than illegal drugs. According to the World Health Organisation, in places such as Australia, Canada, the EU, New Zealand and the USA, tobacco has five times the impact of illegal drugs. The Global Youth Tobacco Survey found that one in seven 13- to 15-year-olds smoked.

DRUNK AND DISORDERLY

Alcohol is not far behind tobacco in the scale of the ill-effects it causes. Regular, heavy drinkers can become physically and emotionally dependent on alcohol, but occasional heavy drinking sessions also take a toll on people's health and can lead to unplanned pregnancies, accidents, fights and crime as people are more likely to act aggressively and take risks when drunk.

A man smokes with his daughter beside him. He may be damaging her health through her passive smoking as well as his own, but it is legal for him to do so.

Two men sleep off the effects of a night's drinking. When they wake, they may well have a headache and nausea – a hangover – caused by too much alcohol.

GET THE FACTS STRAIGHT

- In the UK, 40% of violent offences are committed when offenders are under the influence of alcohol.
- Almost one in ten 12- to 15-year-olds and one in three 16- to 17-year-olds admit arguing, fighting, stealing or committing criminal damage after drinking.
- Industry estimates that £3.6 million is lost to the UK economy owing to people working poorly or taking time off work because of hangovers.
- In Australia, it has been estimated that 70-80% of night-time assaults happen after drinking, and the rates of night-time assaults seem to relate to how much alcohol has been sold locally.

OVER THE LIMIT

Binge-drinking among young people is a big concern in the UK. The average amount drunk by 11- to 15-year-olds doubled between 1990 and 2000. More than half the 15- and 16-year-olds questioned said they had drunk too much at least once in the past month. Yet when someone wants to open an off-licence or shop selling cigarettes in their neighbourhood, parents rarely express concern about the effect on their children and teenagers.

ACCEPTABLE HABITS

Perhaps this is because alcohol and tobacco have long been a part of white, Western culture. Brewing has been around for thousands of years in many cultures. Tobacco came to Europe from the Americas as long ago as the mid-1500s and it spread to many other countries from there. Acceptance of drugs has as much to do with their history as the amount of damage they can do.

PEOPLE IN MANY WESTERN CULTURES are opposed to cannabis because they believe it is harmful, yet they enjoy a drink. In other countries, it is acceptable to smoke cannabis, but not to drink. Attitudes to drugs also change over time: coffee was banned in the Muslim world in the 1500s because of fears about its effects on health.

⬇ *Tunisian Muslims enjoy a coffee together – a social activity similar to meeting for a beer in Western cultures.*

➡ *Rastafarians use ganga (cannabis) in their religious rituals to aid meditation and to make decisions.*

CANNABIS CONSUMPTION

Many Muslims do not drink alcohol on religious grounds. However, in some Muslim countries, cannabis use is more commonly acceptable, although not always legal. Hindus traditionally use cannabis in their festivals. For example during Mahashivratri – when Lord Shiva is believed to have performed *tandava*, the dance of destruction – they consume *bhang* (cannabis extract) and *thandai* (cold milk laced with *bhang*). Not all Hindus approve of this practice.

RASTAFARIANS

Cannabis is central to the religious life of many Rastafarians. In Jamaica, where many Rastafarians live, a government commission has recommended making it legal for adults to use ganga (cannabis) privately and as part of religious rituals. But Jamaica faces pressure from the US government. It fears that legalisation in Jamaica will give American citizens the message that cannabis is harmless.

↑ *Coca leaves for sale in a South American market.*

CHEWING COCA

Coca, from which cocaine is derived, is another plant with a long history of use as a drug. It has been grown for thousands of years in South America and is used to combat fatigue and hunger. Workers, seeking to boost their endurance, stuff their mouths with coca leaves while chewing a substance that releases the drug inside the leaves where it is present at very low levels. The production of cocaine involves concentrating this extract.

A PICK-ME-UP

Opium and its derivatives, heroin and morphine, were widely sold as medicines and pick-me-ups throughout Europe and North America in the 1800s and early 1900s. In the US, housewives were the most common users until people realised that the drugs were addictive and they were banned – apart from some very tightly-controlled medical usage. However, the trade continued and became big business – for those prepared to break the law.

FACING THE ISSUES

Alcohol was banned in the USA from 1920 to 1933 (the Prohibition era) because the huge quantities that were drunk – 27 litres (7 gallons) of pure alcohol per adult per year – were thought to be contributing to crime, poverty and violence. The ban ended because people were concerned about the loss of freedom and perhaps because they had forgotten the damage caused by excessive drinking. The ban also led to an increase in the power of criminal gangs, such as the Mafia, which traded illegally in alcohol. However, the ban did seem to have an effect. After the ban was lifted, drinking increased again but to an average of 7.6 litres (2 gallons) per adult, much lower than before.

WHATEVER *your cultural perspective, the illegal drugs trade is a global one. Many of the drugs consumed in the Western world are produced in developing countries, often desperate for the profits of these "cash crops".*

⬆ Opium poppies are grown in remote areas of Afghanistan which are hard to police, even if the government wants to.

⬇ Rebel troops in Columbia prepare for battle. They rely on the income from drugs to buy their weapons.

AFGHAN POPPIES

One of the few sources of income for war-torn Afghanistan was growing opium poppies for their seeds to be processed into morphine and heroin. According to the US Drug Enforcement Agency (DEA), Afghanistan's former rulers, the Taliban, a hardline Islamic sect, made most of their money from drugs. However, in return for help from the United Nations Drugs Control Programme, the Taliban had ordered the destruction of the poppy fields. This process was halted by the US-led war in Afghanistan following the terrorist attacks on America on September 11 2001. The UNDCP has estimated that in the immediate aftermath of the war, opium cultivation boomed by 1,400%, although work continues to stop it.

GET THE FACTS STRAIGHT

- The United Nations estimates that the drugs trade takes up 8 per cent of world trade – that's 8 per cent of everything bought and sold around the world.

- In 2000, Americans spent about $36 billion on cocaine, $11 billion on marijuana, $10 billion on heroin, $5.4 billion on methamphetamine and $2.4 billion on other illegal substances.

- According to government figures, the illegal drugs trade in the UK is worth £6.6 billion, only slightly less than what is spent on tobacco.

FINANCING WAR

Cocaine is imported from South America, particularly Brazil, Venezuela and Colombia. The farmers there are often poor and can earn more money growing coca plants than food. In Columbia, too, the drugs trade is used by political groups to fund their fighting in an on-going civil war. The government has to stamp out the drugs trade to stay in power, even though some of its political supporters are involved in it.

MANUFACTURERS

But drugs are not always imported. Synthetic drugs can be made anywhere. One of the biggest problems in the US is methamphetamine. This illegal stimulant can be made from medicines containing pseudoephedrine, which relieves colds and allergies. Some 600,000 US citizens are thought to be chronic "meth" users, compared to 300,000 heroin users. To combat the trade, the US regulated the sale of pseudoephedrine, but dealers then resorted to bulk-buying from Canada.

↑ Drug "barons" in Miami have bought millionaires' mansions like this one with the profits made from the illegal drugs trade.

REACHING THE MARKET

The producers benefit from the drugs trade, but the middle-men who bring the drugs to the users make even more. Heroin sells on the street for nearly 60 times the price the farmers sell it at, cocaine 18 times and cannabis about 4 times. The profits from these mark-ups go to Mafia-style crime organisations, who control the dealers on the street.

AT THE END OF THE CHAIN of supply in the drugs trade are the users – the people whose desire to consume drugs creates the market in the first place. Who are they?

A YOUTHFUL MARKET

The European Monitoring Centre for Drugs and Drug Addiction found that most people who use illegal drugs are either experimenting or doing it for a limited period when young. They are likely to be outgoing, like parties and pubs, and have tried alcohol or tobacco early on. Their parents may use drugs or alcohol or tobacco. They may be wealthier than average, although some studies have shown that the opposite is true and unemployment is a factor. Some research indicates that men are more likely to try drugs than women. The vast majority of users stop for various reasons linked to growing up – for example, a regular job, marriage, children, financial responsibilities.

⬆ *A woman snorts cocaine. This drug used to be for the rich but it is now much cheaper and its use has increased.*

➡ *Two young people smoking cannabis. Will they grow out of the habit?*

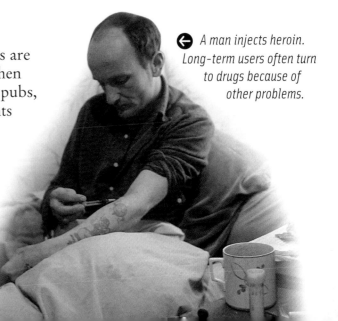

⬅ *A man injects heroin. Long-term users often turn to drugs because of other problems.*

LONG-TERM USE

Long-term, serious drug use tends to happen when a person has had family problems or there is some contributory factor in their physical or mental make-up. They may not think much of themselves or come from a group that is looked down upon by the rest of society. They repeatedly have the chance to take drugs yet they don't have much information about the risks that they are taking. This is perhaps why serious drug abuse often occurs in areas of social deprivation or poverty.

A CHEAPER OPTION

Unsurprisingly, research shows people take drugs because they enjoy them, are curious about their effects or want to rebel against authority. Drugs may seem to offer a break from a rundown environment or traumatic problems. Significantly, many drug users today mention cost as an influence – some illegal drugs are cheaper to buy than alcohol and tobacco because they are not taxed.

FACING THE ISSUES

Singer Boy George spoke frankly about his drug habits in his life story *Take It Like A Man*, which he wrote with Spencer Bright: "I'd always been wary of drugs, of being out of control, but I also had a secret yearning to know what I was missing. My initiation into drugs was so casual, especially after years of pontificating against them. I dropped my first E among friends in a relaxed atmosphere, not in some dingy basement with a bunch of sordid dealers, although I was to meet quite a few of them in the months to come. Coke was a natural progression from E. One led to another, like stepping stones across a murky pond."

CRACKING DOWN

GOVERNMENTS have to decide how they will respond to the illegal drug culture – should they take a softer approach and tolerate some drug usage? Or should they crack down? Either way, governments want to be seen to act to maintain the support of their voters. Countries like the United States have taken the tough line and decided that they should try to stamp out illegal drugs usage altogether. One way of doing this is by stopping the supply.

Soldiers stand by as an illegal crop of coca is destroyed.

US police arrest crack-cocaine dealers.

DESTROYING CROPS

The US government destroys cocaine crops in Columbia by helping its government spray the farms with plant-killing chemicals. This policy has proved effective in the past in countries like Peru. However, it also meant that production in Columbia went up; as Robert Sharpe, of the law reform group Drug Policy Alliance, points out: "Destroy every last coca plant in South America, and domestic [US] methamphetamine production will increase to meet the demand for cocaine-like drugs." Some groups have also objected to spraying on environmental grounds.

PUNISHING THE DEALERS

Many countries rely on harsh penalties against drug-dealing to deter traffickers. Malaysia, Singapore, Saudi Arabia, China and the United States can all execute convicted drug dealers. This rarely happens in the United States, although many people convicted of drugs offences are jailed. A quarter of inmates in state prisons in the USA are there for drug possession.

GET THE FACTS STRAIGHT

- Drug Enforcement Authority figures show drug use has been reduced in the US by 50% overall since the early 1980s.
- Enforcing US drug policy cost $40 billion in 2000 alone.
- In the same year, an estimated 14 million US citizens had used a drug illegally in the past month, according to the Substance Abuse and Mental Health Services Administration.

⬆ *A man is executed for drug dealing in Saudi Arabia.*

HELPING THE USERS

However, US drug users can opt for treatment rather than punishment through the "drug court" system. This allows them to enter a drug treatment programme, and, if they complete it successfully, the charges against them are reduced or dismissed. Other countries have similar programmes, for example the Netherlands and Scotland, which opened its first drug court in 2001. The US laws remain strict though: drug-offenders forfeit welfare benefits for life. They may also be refused an educational grant.

IN EUROPE, *many countries are beginning to reconsider their drug laws, particularly in relation to cannabis. This softer approach is mainly applied to the users rather than the dealers. One of the main arguments for a change in attitude is it frees up police time to deal with the more dangerous or "hard" drugs.*

FINES AND WARNING

In Spain, Italy and Portugal, people found in possession any drugs, including heroin, for their own use may be warned, fined, offered counselling or, as in Italy, have their driving licence suspended. They have broken the law, but they do not face criminal proceedings. In the UK, the law is set to change so that most people caught with a small amount of cannabis on them may not be arrested – the decision lies with individual police officers. In Switzerland, moves to make cannabis legal have begun.

← *People sit outside a discreetly named "coffee shop" in Amsterdam – in reality, a "brown café".*

→ *Cannabis leaves. Many feel this drug should have a similar legal status to tobacco and alcohol.*

GOING DUTCH

Ironically, despite its world-famous "brown cafés" which sell cannabis, drugs possession in the Netherlands remains illegal. The Dutch have a complicated approach, but one which they believe works well. Possession of a small amount of cannabis – under 5 grammes – is tolerated, although all drugs found by the police are confiscated. The sale of drugs is a criminal offence, but once again is tolerated in the case of cannabis if it is sold through the "brown cafés".

PROTECTING THE USER

The Dutch health ministry says that the aim is to protect soft-drug users: "The aim is to keep soft drugs separate from hard drugs in order to protect soft-drug users, especially youngsters who want to try them out, from exposure to hard drugs and the criminal elements who traffic in them." The Dutch include ecstasy among the hard drugs.

CONTROLLED ACCESS

"Brown cafés" have to stick to strict rules that have recently been toughened: they may not sell more than 5 grammes to a customer at any one time; only over-18s can go in; and they can't sell alcohol. If they cause a nuisance, they are closed down. As the panel of statistics shows, this approach seems to be more effective than the US policy. But US officials dispute this, on the grounds that the statistics are not comparable as they were prepared using different criteria.

GET THE FACTS STRAIGHT

- In the Netherlands, about 16% of the population have tried cannabis at some point in their lives, according to a report published in 1999. The US figure for 2001 was 37%.
- The 2001 US and 1999 Dutch figures for trying cocaine and heroin are: cocaine – 12% US, 0.3% Netherlands; heroin – 1.4% US, 0.3% Netherlands.
- Just 2.5% of Dutch citizens said that they had used cannabis in the month preceding the 1999 survey, less than half the 2001 US survey rate.

ANOTHER WAY TO REDUCE the demand for drugs or control their use is through education. The two most common approaches to drugs education are simply described as "Just Say No" and "Just Say Know". The debate over which works best is fierce.

Rachel Whitear at 16. She died of a heroin overdose at 23. Her parents allowed pictures of Rachel's dead body to be published alongside pictures of her before she took heroin in the hope that it would warn other people of the dangers of drugs.

NO RISK

Just Say No was a campaign launched in the 1980s to encourage young people to refuse to have anything to do with drugs. Its supporters believe that the only safe approach is not to take any drugs at all, and that it is putting young people's lives at risk to do anything that might appear to condone drug-taking.

Prince Harry found himself in the media spotlight for using cannabis. After his father found out about his drug use, the young prince was instructed by the police about drugs and the possible consequences of using them.

EDUCATED CHOICE

Many people involved in drugs education feel this approach is too simplistic. They argue that some young people will decide to take drugs however strongly they are warned against them, and they should have information that will help them to reduce the risks. So "Just Say Know" supporters believe young people should be well-informed about the effects of drugs so that they can decide for themselves.

HAVING THE CONFIDENCE

Both approaches sometimes include lessons on self-esteem. An example is the Drug Abuse Resistance Education (DARE), which is run in 54 countries including the US, the UK, Canada and New Zealand. The idea is to give people the confidence to reject peer pressure to take drugs. DrugScope, in the UK, points out that peer pressure can also act in the opposite direction - encouraging people not to take drugs.

The argument about which approach is best looks set to continue: clear figures on which is more effective are hard to come by, and what statistics exist have been disputed.

A police officer instructs US children about drugs in the classroom as part of their drugs education programme.

MEDIA INFLUENCE

Some people are worried that the media portrayal of drugs, including alcohol and cigarettes, also "educates" young people into believing their use is acceptable and safe. The popular Australian teen drama *The Secret Life of Us* has been accused of showing alcohol consumption too often without sufficiently emphasising its negative consequences. A researcher from Melbourne University found that all the characters in the programme drank alcohol and it appeared in a quarter of all scenes. In reality a fifth of young Australians do not drink at all. However, the research did not seek to establish whether more teenagers started to drink as a result of watching the programme.

WHAT DO YOU THINK?

- Do you think there should be drugs education in schools?
- If so, at what age do you think drugs education should begin?
- Which message works best: "Just Say No" or "Just Say Know"? Why?
- How do shocking images of drug misuse affect you?
- Who should talk to you about drugs: parents, teachers, the police, drug therapy workers?
- Is your opinion about drugs influenced by your friends?
- How are you influenced by the way legal and illegal drugs are portrayed on TV or in the movies?

KICKING THE HABIT

THERE ARE MANY government schemes and drugs organisations set up to help get people through the physical and mental trauma of coming off drugs. It is seen as a way of containing and hopefully lowering drug misuse.

WITHDRAWAL SYMPTOMS

Heavy users find coming off drugs hard. They feel ill as their body is not used to functioning without the drug. Symptoms vary depending on the extent of drug use, but may include feelings of nausea, shaking, cold sweats. In extreme cases, withdrawal can lead to a coma or even death. Addicts can also struggle to face the world and their problems without the cushion of the drug.

This man at a night club offers to test ecstasy tablets for dangerous additives.

The Swiss allowed drug-users to buy and use drugs without police intervention in a park in Zurich. But "needle park" attracted drug addicts from far and wide. It was closed and replaced by more hygienic drug consumption rooms.

HOW TO HELP

Some schemes involve giving frequent users, usually of heroin, alternative drugs such as methadone on prescription. Methadone is addictive in itself and is given under medical supervision. However, its use is thought to wean addicts off heroin or to stop their habit from getting worse. A study of a methadone treatment programme in London also found that users committed 74% less crime to fund their habit. Results like this have caused some governments to experiment with giving addicts free heroin.

HARM REDUCTION

Some governments controversially recognise that some addicts will not stop using drugs so they should be helped to take drugs safely. Schemes exist where addicts who inject drugs can get clean needles in exchange for used ones that might spread blood-borne diseases, such as HIV and hepatitis B and C. In Australia, Switzerland and some EU countries, facilities exist where addicts can inject drugs under medical supervision. The aim is to reduce the number of fatal overdoses.

A SAFE TEST?

Pill-testing is offered by some groups such as DanceSafe in the US. This helps users to tell if harmful chemicals have been used to make the pills, but they can't test for everything or take into account individual reactions. US teenager Nicole Crowder took the same type of ecstasy pill as her friends. They were OK; she died.

Drug addicts pray together as part of their therapy at a Christian drug rehabilitation centre.

FACING THE ISSUES

Frequently, people dependent on drugs have an aspect to their personality that makes them prone to addiction. As heroin-addict Rachel puts it: "My drugs were heroin, crack, cannabis, tranquillisers, anything. Drink. But I can see addictive behaviour in me long before the drugs came along. That was just a symptom. My addiction can come out in other ways: in food, in relationships." Rachel came to recognise this while attending a treatment programme to come off heroin. These programmes usually offer addicts the chance to talk though their problems individually or in a group with other users in order to find ways of coping without drugs.
[Source: *The Observer*]

THE MOST RADICAL *solution to the drug problem is legalisation – removing practically all penalties for drugs. This idea finds many sympathisers, particularly in relation to cannabis. However there is also strong opposition. Here, simply, are the main arguments for and against.*

PRO: PERSONAL CHOICE

It is a personal decision whether someone takes drugs. The authorities have no right to interfere if no-one else is being harmed. If drugs were used openly, then society would develop informal rules for their use.

PRO: SAVING MONEY

In Canada, it is estimated that $475 million a year is spent by the federal authorities on enforcing drugs laws. Other countries face similarly big bills. If drug laws were dropped, that money could be saved. This argument is also used for partial legalisation: if cannabis was legal, police could concentrate their activities elsewhere (see page 20).

PRO: BETTER CONTROL

Keeping drugs illegal creates dangers. Without a legal quality check, dealers can spin their supply of drugs out by mixing – "cutting" – them with other, sometimes harmful, materials so they can make more money. If drugs were legal, it would also mean that people did not have to go to criminals to buy them. Governments could also control use through taxation. It is hard to control and regulate a trade that exists outside of the law.

PRO: CANNABIS

Alcohol, a legal drug, makes people aggressive and violent; cannabis does not. It is claimed that cannabis leads onto other drugs, but alcohol and tobacco are usually the first drugs that people try. Cannabis is no more dangerous than legal drugs, so governments are operating double-standards. Cannabis also has medical uses for which it should be made legal.

⬅ *Two protesters demand the legalisation of cannabis, making fun of people who suggest it is a dangerous drug.*

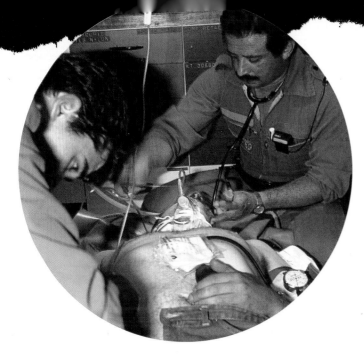

⬅ *Would legalisation of drugs add to the medical costs caused by drug misuse?*

AGAINST: CANNABIS

Most people who become dependent on hard drugs, such as heroin, begin their drug use with cannabis, but cannabis is also dangerous in itself (see page 7). It is a myth that cannabis makes you mellow: youths who use cannabis weekly are four times more likely to behave violently than those who do not. There is no medical need for cannabis to be legalised as there are legal alternatives available, for example Marinol.

AGAINST: EXPERIENCE

Existing "softer" approaches have not proved entirely successful. The Netherlands is troubled by drug "tourists" and has become the primary EU country for ecstasy production. Sweden and Alaska both experimented with relaxed drug laws; drug use increased so the laws were tightened again.

AGAINST: NO PROTECTION

Governments have a responsibility to protect their citizens from the dangers of drugs – in particular the most vulnerable, who are most likely to be tempted. Simply, if drugs were made legal then far more people would use them. Public concern over alcohol has not kept its use at a low level – so why do people think that peer pressure will stop drugs becoming even more of a problem?

AGAINST: COSTS INCREASE

Alcohol and tobacco cost society because of the illness and anti-social behaviour they produce. Legalising drugs would only add to this.

AGAINST: A NEW ILLEGAL TRADE

If drugs became legal, governments would probably be forced by the alcohol and tobacco industries to tax them in line with drinks and cigarettes. So, just as there is an illegal trade in cheap, tax-free alcohol and tobacco, an illegal trade in tax-free drugs would also be created. Money saved on policing illegal drugs would then go on stopping this tax dodge.

⬇ Legal drugs would still be sold illegally to avoid paying tax.

THERE IS A THEORY that the market for drugs fluctuates like that of any commodity that is bought and sold. Eventually everyone who wants to try drugs has done so. As a result, for a while at least, the market dies away regardless of government policy.

A DECLINE IN USERS

The European Monitoring Centre for Drugs and Drugs Addiction has suggested this as a reason why the number of 15- and 16-year-olds who had tried cannabis fell in the UK and Ireland: from 41% to 35% in the UK and from 37% to 32% in Ireland in the period 1995-99. They were the only EU countries where this trend happened and they had been the two nations with the highest rates of use. The use of other illegal drugs in the two countries also reduced: a 10% drop in the UK and a 7% drop in Ireland over the same period.

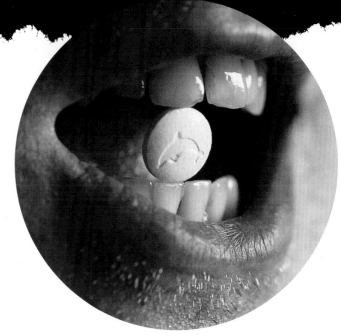

→ *Ecstasy tablets are branded like other fashion items. Will their use eventually fall out of fashion as well?*

→ *At some point, most of us will be offered drugs, legal or illegal. In the end, the decision to take them is our own.*

WHAT DO YOU THINK?

- Should governments try to curb drug use or are they wasting their time?
- Would you be more likely to take drugs if they were legal?
- What effect do you think this would have on you, your family and friends and your community?

RISE AND FALL

Researchers talk about drugs use coming in waves. Like an epidemic, it peaks and then dies back down. One theory for this is that when drugs use reaches high levels, people see the damage it causes. Drugs are then rejected by many sectors of society and their use falls. This attitude persists for a few decades, but eventually the consequences are forgotten and people develop an interest in drugs again.

TAKING ACTION

But governments do not want to wait for this to happen. In Europe, attention is increasingly focusing on drug-dealers, rather than drug-purchasers. The US continues to clamp down on users: a government lawyer suggested that every US high school pupil could be drugs-tested under existing laws. In New Zealand, moves to legalise cannabis stalled, but more towns are introducing alcohol-free zones. Police say rowdy behaviour has been halved.

NO CLEAR PATH

Which is right: a tough policy, a more liberal attitude or a different approach for each drug? The European Monitoring Centre for Drugs and Drug Addiction found that countries with liberal drug policies, such as the Netherlands, had similar rates of drug use to countries with stricter policies, for example, Sweden. There are no easy answers. One thing is sure: drugs will remain part of our culture, at times more significant than others, and so too will the debate on how to live with them.

GLOSSARY

addiction: Psychological and often also physical dependence on a drug.

cannabis: The plant that is used to make the drug hashish, from the flower resin, and the drug marijuana, made from its leaves.

cocaine: A strong stimulant drug derived from the coca plant, which comes in a powder form.

coke: Short for cocaine.

commodity: Something that can be bought and sold.

crack: A very strong form of cocaine that has been crystallised and is smoked.

criminal proceedings: These begin with an arrest and may be followed by a formal warning or a court case.

depressants: Substances which dull pain. They relax people and slow their reactions and heart beat, sometimes dangerously.

drug court: A court set up to deal with people charged with a drugs crime or criminals who have a drugs problem. They enable the accussed to enter treatment programmes as an alternative to punishment.

E: Short for ecstasy.

ecstasy: The common street name for the artificial stimulant drug whose chemical name is methylene dioxy-methamphetamine (MDMA). Taking MDMA is sometimes called "dropping an e".

illicit: Illegal or disapproved of by most of society.

hallucinogens: Drugs that change the way that your brain operates so you "hallucinate", that is you believe things are happening that are not.

harm minimisation: Things that can be done to reduce the damage that people can do to themselves through drugs.

heroin: A depressant drug made from the opium poppy. It is smoked or injected and is highly addictive.

magic mushrooms: A variety of small, bell-shaped fungi eaten by some drug users for its hallucinogenic effect.

marijuana: A drug made from the leaves of the cannabis plant.

methamphetamine: A synthetic stimulant drug that produces a "high" similar to that of cocaine.

morphine: An opium-derived drug used in medicine as a pain-killer.

off-licence: A shop licensed to sell alcohol to be drunk elsewhere, not in the shop itself.

prostitute: Someone who sells sex for money.

solvent: A chemical found in certain household products, such as some glues, which if sniffed acts as a depressant drug.

sports drugs: These drugs can be used illicitly to increase muscle size, speed or strength.

stimulants: Drugs that make users feel energetic and bubbly. They increase the heart rate and blood pressure, sometimes dangerously.

synthetic: Describes drugs that have been manufactured, rather than plant-based drugs.

trafficking: Distributing and selling something, particularly on an international basis.

tolerance: If a drug is used regularly, the body adapts to its presence. To get the same effect, the user has to take more of the drug. The user has developed a tolerance.

withdrawal symptoms: The unpleasant feelings and ill-health that someone experiences when they stop taking a drug on which they are dependent.

FURTHER INFORMATION

AUSTRALIA

Alcohol and Drug Foundation
A community organisation concerned with minimising the problems associated with drugs.
www.naturalhigh.org
PO Box 332, Spring Hill, QLD 4004
TEL: 07 3832 3798

Australian Drug Foundation
A not-for-profit organisation that works to prevent and reduce alcohol and drug misuse.
www.somazone.com.au
PO Box 818, North Melbourne, VIC 3051
TEL: 03 927 88100

Kids Help Line, Australia
A general helpline for 5- to 18-year-olds. This free, confidential service was founded by a Catholic brotherhood.
www.kidshelp.com.au
PO Box 376, Red Hill QLD 4059
TEL: 1800 551800 (free in Australia)

NEW ZEALAND

Foundation for Alcohol and Drug Education
Organisation offering education and training on health and safety.
www.fade.org.nz
PO Box 33-1505
Takapuna, Auckland
TEL: 09 488 1298

Drug Arm NZ
A Christian organisation promoting a healthy lifestyle without the use of unnecessary drugs.
Tauranga TEL: 07 577 0675
Auckland TEL: 09 814 8943

Drug Abuse Resistance Education (DARE)
An education programme on drugs and violence prevention, available in New Zealand and many other countries. Their website links with both the UK and US branches of DARE.
www.dare.org.nz
PO Box 50744, Porirua
TEL: 04 238 9550

UK

Crew 2000
A coalition of club-goers and others who do not condone or condemn drug use, but offer information on steps that can be taken to reduce potential harm.
www.crew2000.co.uk
32/32a Cockburn St., Edinburgh, EH1 1PB
TEL: 0131 220 3404

DrugScope
A leading UK centre of expertise on drugs with international links.
www.drugscope.org.uk
Waterbridge House
32-26 Loman Street, London SE1 0EE
TEL: 020 7928 1211

Health Promotion England
Government-sponsored information on drugs, alcohol and treatment.
Illegal drugs
www.trashed.co.uk
Alcohol
www.wrecked.co.uk

UK National Drugs Helpline
Freephone UK 0800 77 66 00

USA

Partnership for a Drug-Free America
A coalition of media and entertainment professionals with the aim of persuading young people to reject drugs.
www.drugfreeamerica.org
405 Lexington Avenue, Suite 1601, New York, NY 10174

DanceSafe
A group promoting health and safety within the rave and nightclub community.
www.dancesafe.org
c/o HRC,
22 West 27th St., 5th floor, New York, NY 10011

National Youth Anti-Drug Media Campaign
Launched by the White House's Office of National Drug Control Policy with the aim of keeping children and young people drug-free.
www.theantidrug.com

INDEX